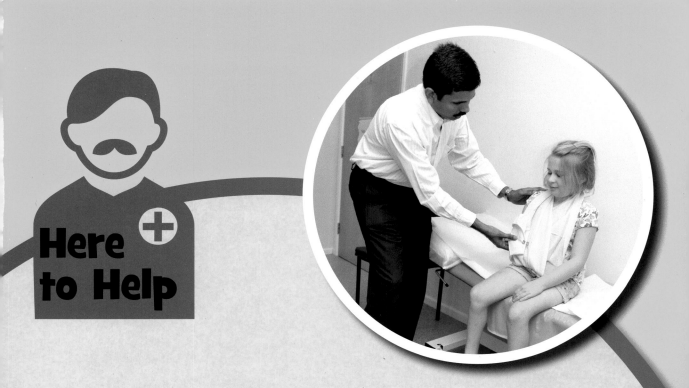

Here to Help

DOCTOR

Hannah Phillips

Photography by Bobby Humphrey

W

FRANKLIN WATTS
LONDON · SYDNEY

Franklin Watts
First published in Great Britain in 2015 by the Watts Publishing Group

Credits
Series Editors: Hannah Phillips and Paul Humphrey
Series Designer: D. R. ink
Photographer: Bobby Humphrey
Produced for Franklin Watts by Discovery Books Ltd.

Dewey number: 610.6'95
HB ISBN: 978 1 4451 3991 3
Library ebook ISBN: 978 1 4451 3992 0

Printed in China

Franklin Watts
An imprint of
Hachette Children's Group
Part of the Watts Publishing Group
Carmelite House
50 Victoria Embankment
London EC4Y 0DZ

An Hachette UK company
www.hachette.co.uk

www.franklinwatts.co.uk

The publisher and packager would like to thank the following people for their help and involvement with the book: Dr Mani, Mark Pritchard, Jo Erskine, Rose Thomas, Padmini Mukundapriya and all other staff at the Bobblestock surgery in Hereford. We would also like to thank the patients who took part for their cooperation.

Contents

Words in **bold** are in the glossary on page 24.

I am a doctor

Hello, my name is Doctor Manikandan, but all my **patients** call me Doctor Mani. It is my job to help people who are ill or injured.

I see lots of patients every day.

Hello!

?

What is your doctor's name?

I start work at 8:00am. I tell Kate that I am here. Kate is a **receptionist** at the **surgery**.

Kate greets everybody who comes into the surgery. She takes phone calls from patients and makes **appointments** on her computer.

Meet the team

There are other medical staff at this **practice**. They all have different jobs to do.

Jo is a **nurse**. She helps us by taking **blood tests** and giving health advice to patients.

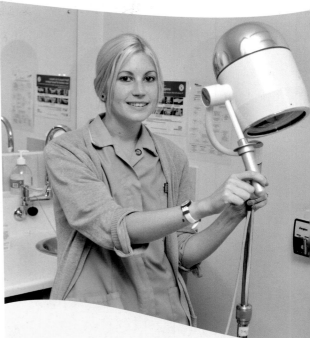

Rachel is a **health care assistant**. She helps the doctors to prepare for minor operations.

Rosie is the **counsellor**. She helps people who are worried about their illness or injuries.

Padmini is a **newly qualified doctor**. She is still training, but will see some of my patients to gain more experience.

?

Why do you think there are different types of medical staff at the surgery?

Mark is the practice **manager**. It is his job to make sure that everything runs smoothly.

Getting ready

I go to my room and check my computer for emails and today's appointments.

It's going to be a busy day!

I check I have all my equipment ready.

Thermometer – I use this for checking body temperature.

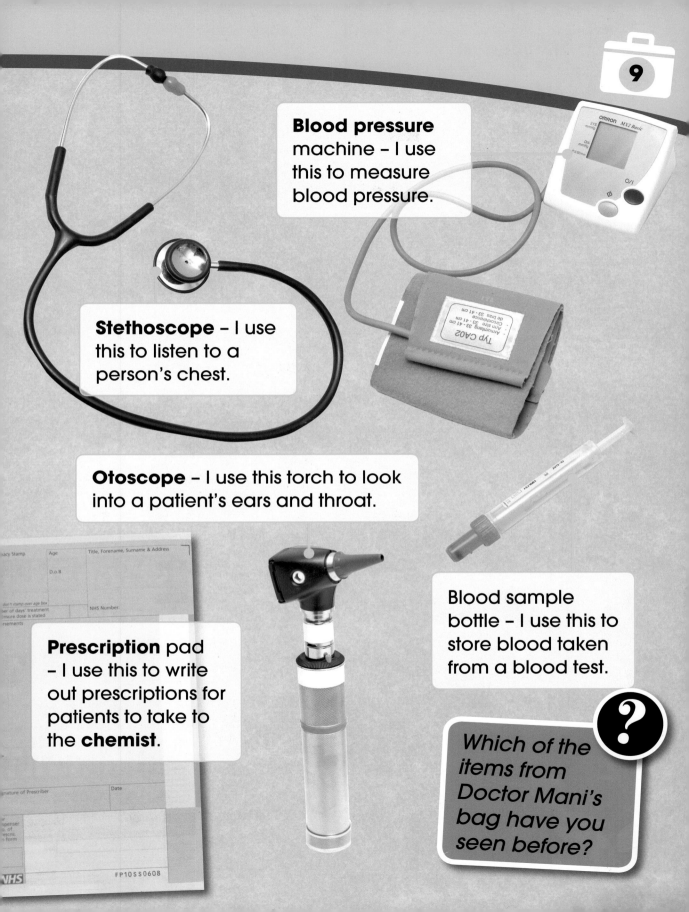

Blood pressure machine – I use this to measure blood pressure.

Stethoscope – I use this to listen to a person's chest.

Otoscope – I use this torch to look into a patient's ears and throat.

Prescription pad – I use this to write out prescriptions for patients to take to the **chemist**.

Blood sample bottle – I use this to store blood taken from a blood test.

? Which of the items from Doctor Mani's bag have you seen before?

The patients arrive

The first patients arrive at 8:30am.

They sign in using the touchscreen in reception.
This tells the doctor that their patient is here.

In the waiting room there are magazines to read and toys for children.

There are also information posters on the walls for people to look at.

Why do you think there are posters in the doctor's waiting room?

?

Walking

Walking is a great way of getting around. Not only does it have fantastic benefits to help improve your health and fitness, you'll be protecting the environment by reducing your carbon footprint and the icing on the cake is that it's free. All you need is a comfortable pair of shoes, and on the odd occasion a waterproof coat or umbrella just in case it rains.

For most people walking can be easily incorporated into a daily routine, for example you can walk to work, school or the shops. If it's too far to walk all the way then catch a bus and get off a few stops earlier. You'll soon feel healthier and notice the positive impact on your finances.

Walking is a very safe form of exercise, however, if you have any health problems or concerns please consult your GP.

Don't run before you can walk! Walking is more likely to become a lifelong habit if you build up the distance you walk gradually. Set yourself weekly or monthly goals. You could even keep a travel diary to record how far you walk and the time it takes for regular journeys, that way you can monitor your progress.

Contact your local council to see if they have walking or cycling maps so you can plan your journey effectively.

Did you know...

27% of all trips are less than 1 mile long, 17% of these are made by car.

Walking on a regular basis can help prevent and reduce the risk of: cardiovascular disease (CVD), cancer, obesity, diabetes, stroke, mental health problems, high blood pressure and musculoskeletal health – osteoporosis and osteoarthritis.

Walking helps relieve stress and elevate your mood.

Walking reduces levels of cholesterol in your blood and can lower high blood pressure.

Walking improves efficiency of your heart and lungs.

On average, every minute of walking can extend your life by 1.5 to 2 minutes. That's about a 2 for 1 trade-off!

Walking promotes healthier skin due to increased circulation.

At an average pace, walking 1 mile takes approximately 20 minutes.

Walking is great for your health

My first patient

I go to the waiting room to call my first patient.

Toney has a sore throat and a temperature.

Tell me where it hurts.

? How do you feel when you have to visit the doctor?

I use my otoscope to **examine** his throat.

I check his **tonsils** to see if they are **infected**.

Say 'Ahhh'.

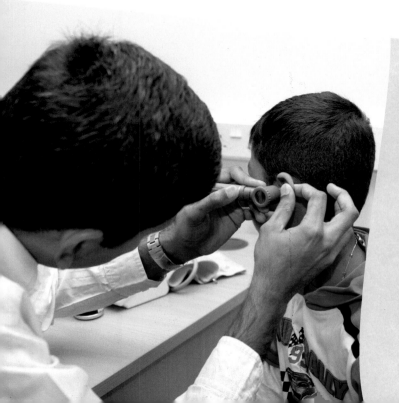

I check Toney's ears using the otoscope too.

Toney's tonsils are badly infected. I write a prescription for Toney's dad to take to the chemist.

Sprained shoulder

Charlotte has a **sprained** shoulder. Her arm is in a **sling** to help it **heal**.

How does it feel today?

?

Have you ever sprained a part of your body or even broken a bone? How did it feel?

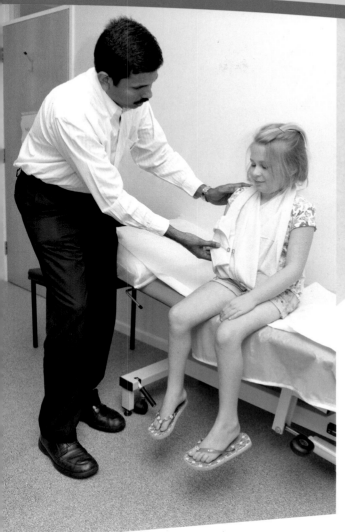

I examine Charlotte's arm to see if she can move it easily. She tells me it still hurts a little when I move it.

I show her a picture of where she has sprained her shoulder. She needs to wear her sling for another week so her shoulder can heal.

Home visit

I have a home visit to do today because an elderly patient is unable to get to the surgery. I make sure that I have the equipment I need in my doctor's bag.

I arrive at my patient's house, and knock on the door.

This patient has a bad cough and a chest infection. I use the stethoscope to check her heartbeat.

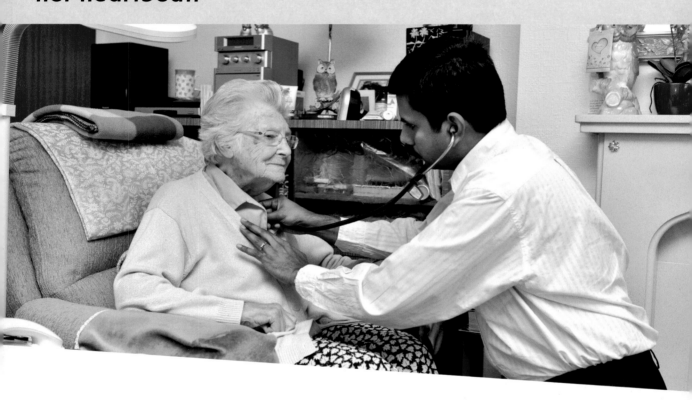

I also check her blood pressure to make sure it is not too high or too low.

She needs lots of rest to help her get better.

Minor operation

My next appointment is back at the surgery. A patient has a **mole** that needs to be removed.

Moles are very common and are usually harmless. But it is important to get them checked by a doctor if they change shape or size.

I prepare for the operation by washing my hands thoroughly. I put on my gloves.

?

Why do doctors have to wash their hands before performing an operation?

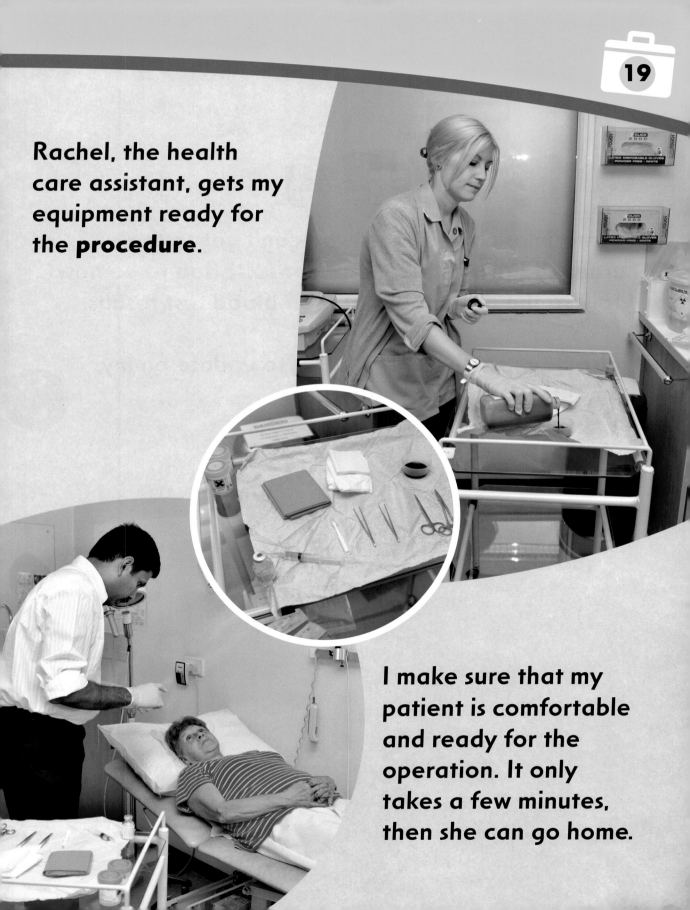

Rachel, the health care assistant, gets my equipment ready for the **procedure**.

I make sure that my patient is comfortable and ready for the operation. It only takes a few minutes, then she can go home.

End of the day

I sometimes call patients who can't get to the surgery. I have a telephone **consultation** to do now. I talk to the patient about their blood test results.

I also have some patient notes to update on my computer from today's surgery.

?

Why do you think it's easier to have patient notes on a computer than on paper?

There is no need to worry!

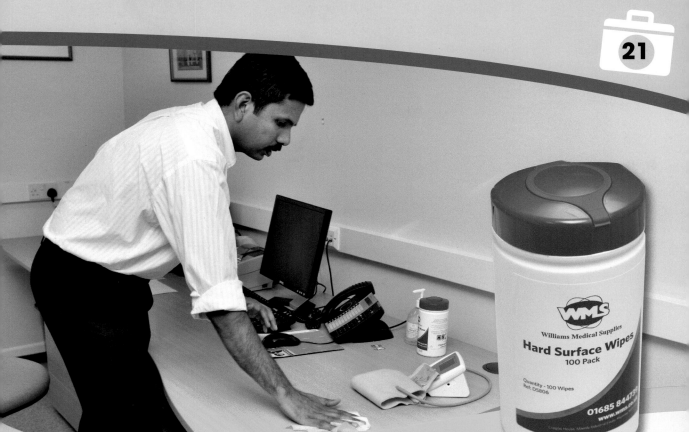

I wipe down my desk at the end of the day to make sure it is clean. **Hygiene** is important because **bacteria** can be harmful.

It is 6:00pm and time for me to go home.

Helping people

I really enjoy my job as a doctor. Most of all, I enjoy helping people get better when they are sick and helping them stay healthy.

I enjoy being a doctor.

When you grow up...

If you would like to be a doctor here are some simple tips and advice.

What kind of person are you?

- You are friendly and you would like to help people get better
- You are interested in the body and how it works
- Most of all, you enjoy helping people.

How do you become a doctor?

To become a doctor you will have to study science subjects at GCSE (Scottish Standard Grades) and at A Level (Scottish Highers). You will also have to study Medicine at university.

Answers

P7. There are different types of medical staff at the surgery because they all do different jobs and treat people with different kinds of medical problems.

P11. The posters tell people how to keep themselves fit and healthy.

P18. Doctor's wash their hands before surgery to get rid of any harmful bacteria.

P20. It's easier to have patient notes on a computer instead of on paper because they can be easily changed every time a patient visits the surgery.

Were your answers the same as the ones in this book? Don't worry if they were different, sometimes there is more than one right answer. Talk about your answer with other people. Can you explain why you think your answer is right?

Glossary

appointments arrangements to be somewhere at a set time

bacteria small, living things that can harm you

blood pressure the rate at which your blood moves around your body

blood test when a doctor takes a small amount of blood to test for disease

chemist a place where you go to get medicine, or the person who gives you medicine

consultation another name for a meeting or a telephone discussion with a doctor

counsellor someone who helps people get over problems

examine to look at something closely

heal to get better

health care assistant someone trained to help a doctor in his or her surgery

hygiene cleanliness; keeping clean

infected attacked by germs or bacteria

manager someone who takes care of the day-to-day running of an organisation

mole a small, raised area on the skin

newly qualified doctor a doctor who has just passed their medical exams and is still training

nurse a qualified medical assistant who looks after sick or injured people

otoscope an instrument with a light and lenses to help doctors look inside the body

patients sick or injured people

practice another name for a doctor's surgery

prescription an order for medicine

procedure another name for an operation

receptionist someone who welcomes people into an office

sling a loop of cloth worn over the shoulder to support an injured arm

sprained describes a damaged joint

stethoscope an instrument used by doctors to listen to a person's heart and lungs

surgery the place where a doctor works; also another name for an operation

thermometer an instrument used by doctors to take a person's temperature

tonsils the two soft lumps at the back of your throat; they swell up if you have an infection in them

Index